The **GOO**

Evangelist Joyce Houseman

Kalamazoo "Tipper News" Articles

By Evangelist Joyce Houseman

Evangelist Joyce Houseman's "Tipper News" articles: Compiled and published by daughter, Carol (Houseman) Gebert.

Tipper News began publishing circa 1960. By 1974 it was published by Kalamazoo Publishing Co. It was a bi-weekly.

Scriptures: King James Version of the Holy Bible: Public Domain in the USA.

Pictures: Pixabay.com

Joyce Houseman's music can be ordered from Carol Gebert at carolegebert@gmail.com

"The Good Word" Printed in the USA in the year of 2015

Contact information: carolegebert@gmail.com

Galen and Joyce Houseman

In loving memory of Joyce Houseman, Composer, Vocalist, Recording Artist, Multi-Instrumentalist, Public Speaker, Minister, Author of Books, Articles, Plays... And the best mother and grandmother, her children and grandchildren ever could have hoped for.

"Your Word Is A Lamp
For My Feet And A
Light On My Path."
Psalm119:105

THE GOOD WORD

By Evangelist Joyce Houseman

"A True Story"

The following is a true story about a man named Ted. His prison number was 24061. Ted was only fourteen-years-old when he was well on his way to securing that number. A confirmed alcoholic, his mind became confused as he drank "Sneaky Pete" (wine) and smoked pot. He could not distinguish real from make believe.

Ted was one of nine children, in his broken, poverty-stricken home. His home setting filled him with hate, prejudice and envy. Jobs were not available for fourteen-year-old boys so Ted turned to stealing for supporting his drinking and drug addictions. Purse snatching; rolling drunks, shoplifting, and robbing homes, made him the leader of a gang of many things.

The law was never far behind him, and he began a series of jail stays. He was sentenced to a school for boys and was in and out of the school three times. Bitterness and loneliness consumed him. Ted's mother's prayers for him, were unceasing! He tried to escape the things of the world by becoming a Christian, but it did not last. The pull of the world was too strong! He spent years running from God. His adult years brought jail time; three children, a broken marriage, and self-hatred. A car accident brought him to the brink of death. Near death, he thought of his Christian mother and her faithfulness in visiting him in jails and prison. Tears for Ted were always in her eyes. God spared Ted's life, but running from God, had not yet reached its climax. Four days of drinking led him to the unthinkable! In a drunken state of mind, he argued with a friend. The argument led to three bullets going into his friend... killing him!

Ted had reached a point of no return. In prison, he prayed, but his prayers did not go far. He was filled with self-pity. Ted finally took a good look at himself. He did not like what he saw. He said, "God break me; tear me apart, give me a new heart, and a part in your Kingdom." After prayer and tears, he got up, and for the first time, his old ways were washed away by the blood of Jesus.

After serving his sentence, he was released from prison a new man! He started a new life as a worker for Christ. He became the head of a half-way house, where he worked with countless numbers of troubled men. The devil's point of no return was turned by the grace of God! For the first time, Ted experienced life in a way that he had never known before. Your situation may or may not be the same as Ted's, but whatever it might be, God can do the same for you!

THE GOOD WORD

By Evangelist Joyce Houseman

"FEAR"

There are two kinds of fear. One is a good kind; the other is not! The Bible tells us that "The fear of the Lord is the beginning of wisdom." (Psalm 111:10). The other fear brings torment. The Bible tells us that many people will die of heart failure in the last days because of fear.

The fear of God is described as reverence and awe toward Him. These fears cause us to walk more carefully. The Bible tells us in Psalm 34, "That the angel of the Lord camps around them that fear God." The Bible also says: "Oh fear the Lord, ye His saints, for there is no want to them that fear Him."

Many people are tormented all their life, by fear of death or by real and imagined fears. David said: "I sought the Lord and He heard me and delivered me, from all of my fears." (Psalm 34).Tormenting fear should not have a part in the life and mind of Christians.

If tormenting fear is in a life; some heart searching needs to be done. "There is no fear in love, but perfect love casts out fear because fear involves torment. But he who fears has not been made perfect in love." (1 John 4:18).

8

THE GOOD WORD

By Evangelist Joyce Houseman

"God's Presence"

Recently, my three-year-old grandson attended Sunday School. His teacher told the children that everyone can do something for God. She asked the children to volunteer their ideas. Robert promptly raised his hand! With great exuberance he said, "I know, I can take God fishing with me." Such a simple, child-like statement, and yet, what a wonderful truth.

We fail to realize that God desires to go with us where ever we go. Abraham Lincoln expressed his need for the presence of God when he began his presidency. He knew that without God, he would fail! With God, he would succeed! Moses knew that his task to deliver Israel would be impossible without God's presence. He sought God, and God gave him the answer: "My presence shall go with thee, and I shall give thee rest." (Exodus 33:14).

Wise people ask God to go with them every day! Vacationers, workers, worshipers, and yes, fishermen ask God's presence to be with them. A songwriter said, "He walks with me, and He talks with me, and He tells me, 'I am His own.' What a joy we share as we tarry there, none other is ever known." (Austin Miles)

THE GOOD WORD

By Evangelist Joyce Houseman

"He eats with Publicans and Sinners"

People wondered at Jesus selection of friends and disciples. The disciples were referred to as ignorant and unlearned men. Why didn't He go to the nearest seminary of the day? Students of theology would have been a fine pick! They might have given Jesus some earthly prestige, and a better reputation.

Jesus even befriended a woman caught in adultery. He defended her against all the men in town. Zacchaeus was a sinner, yet, Jesus invited himself to dinner at his home. Jesus cast seven devils out of Mary Magdalene; she became one of His dearest friends. Jesus said: "Those that are forgiven much, love much!" (Luke 7:47).

Even on the cross, Jesus did not separate himself from the wicked. He told the thief, He would see Him in paradise. After His death and resurrection, Paul, a persecutor of the church; and a killer of Christians, was signaled out to become an Apostle. He was used tremendously for the glory of God! Things might have gone easier for Jesus if He had connected with people of power, but Jesus sees things in people, that no one else can see. I am so glad He does!

THE GOOD WORD

By Evangelist Joyce Houseman

"Humble Thyself"

Israel was persistent; they wanted a King! God was their King, but they were not satisfied. They wanted more. In answer to their desire, God instructed Samuel to anoint Saul, King of Israel. Saul was head and shoulders above everyone in Israel. For a time, he was a good king; but something happened. Saul became proud and turned from God's commandments.

"Pride goes before destruction, And a haughty spirit before a fall." (Proverbs 16:18). Saul disobeyed God. He lied and blamed the people for his disobedience. Samuel spoke to Paul: "When you were little in your own eyes, were you not the head of the tribes of Israel?" (1 Samuel 15:17). Saul had reached the highest position as king, but that day, the Kingdom was rent from him.

God told Samuel to go to the house of Jessie, and anoint one of his sons to be king. There is always someone else who God can use. Our life is useful when we are humble and obedient to God. Scripture says: "God hates a proud look." "Humble yourself in the sight of the Lord, and He will lift you up." (James 4:10). Humility is such a frail and delicate thing; he who thinks he has it, shows by that single thought; he has it not!

11

THE GOOD WORD

By Evangelist Joyce Houseman

"In Your Patience, Possess Ye Your Souls"

Luke 21, gives us a clear description of the days we are living in, and the destructive forces coming upon the earth. False Christ shall come; nations shall rise against nations. There will continue to be wars, earthquakes, famines, and pestilence. There will be signs in the sky.

Christians will be persecuted and cast into prison. While there, people will turn to them for a testimony. Christ said: "Do not be concerned; I will give you the words to say." Many will be betrayed by friends, family, and fellow church-goers. In all of this; Jesus said: "Not a hair of your head shall perish."

Remember this: "In patience, possess ye your souls!" It is patience that will see us through. We have a great need for patience. The Bible says: "Tribulation works patience." (Romans 5:3). Almost everyone has been through trying times. Tough times will give us patience.

Recently, my outgoing mail was stolen and destroyed. Nine articles for this column were destroyed. This article is a result of having that experience. I am learning patience too! Thank God for the trials; they are teaching us patience.

THE GOOD WORD

By Evangelist Joyce Houseman

"New Year or New Life"

The beginning of a New Year reminds us of the new beginnings that we have had in our life. New jobs; new homes, new relationships... Each new beginning creates a desire to make things better. The New Year brings a time of soul searching. For that reason, New Year resolutions are made. Overcoming habits, losing weight, attending church... Many resolutions fail before the month of January is over.

There is a new beginning that can be attained and kept for all of eternity! "Therefore, if anyone is in Christ, he is a new creation; old things have passed away; behold, all things have become new." (11 Corinthians 5:17). Apostle Paul was a perfect example of a new life. He said: "The things I once hated, I now love; and the things I once loved, I now hate!" A personal contact with Jesus Christ changed his life!

It was no longer Paul, but the Spirit of Christ that lived in him. His desires changed! Instead of being an enemy of the cross of Christ; Paul became a friend of Christ. A resolution to rid ourselves of old habits does not always last. Start a new life in Christ; that is a new beginning that will last forever!

13

THE GOOD WORD

By Evangelist Joyce Houseman

"Our Refuge"

God is our refuge and strength, a very present help in trouble. Therefore we will not fear, even though the earth be removed, and though the mountains be carried into the midst of the sea; though its waters roar and be troubled, though the mountains shake with its swelling." (Psalm 46:1-3).

This is a tremendous promise that God has given His children; deliverance, protection and strength in times of distress. There is a secret, however; the fulfillment of the promise has something to do with our dwelling place. Psalm 91 says, "We must dwell in the shadow of the Almighty!" We need to walk very close to Him if we want to be in His shadow. Only then, can He become our fortress and refuge!

The disciples of Christ were guilty at times of following Him from afar off. It was during those times that they got themselves into trouble. There are many things that can come between God and us when we do not stay close to Him. We began to lose faith and become discouraged. Sometimes sin enters our lives and makes the gap that much further apart. A Christian can stay close to the Lord by not neglecting Bible reading and study, and by not neglecting prayer and meditation. We need to fellowship with the saints of God, as well. If we are too busy to pray and read God's Word; we are "too" busy! We need to slow down and remember where our priorities need to be.

It is important to find time to be alone with the Lord. Even Christ left the crowds, so He could fellowship with his father alone. Promises to everyone who abides close to the Lord, are endless! The benefits are tremendous as well! I would like to encourage you to seek after that secret place that is close to God. The Lord said, "You will find me, when you seek for me, with all your heart!"

THE GOOD WORD

By Evangelist Joyce Houseman

"Peace"

Jesus said, "Peace I leave with you, my peace I give unto you. Let not your heart be troubled, neither let it be afraid." (John 14:27). Jesus spoke these words shortly before he went to the cross. The promise of peace was also declared at Jesus' birth. The angels said, "Peace on earth; good will toward men." Peace is a wonderful gift, yet it seems impossible to attain in today's world.

The Bible tells us that peace is something that has to be sought after. "Seek peace and pursue it." (Psalms 34:14). The Bible also tells us that sin and disobedience keep us from peace. There are wonderful promises that we can have when we live our lives for the Lord. "Thou wilt keep him in perfect peace, whose mind is stayed on thee: because he trusts in thee." (Isaiah 26:3).

"God has not given us a spirit of fear but of power and of love and of a sound mind." (2 Timothy 1:7). We can have peace of mind even in the midst of turmoil, because "God is the author of PEACE!" (1 Corinthians 14:43).

16

THE GOOD WORD

By Evangelist Joyce Houseman

"REST"

"Rest in Peace" is often engraved on grave markers. Almost everyone would like to have rest, but they believe it will only come after they die. The Bible says, "Come unto me, all ye that labor and are heavy laden, and I will give you rest. Take my yoke upon you, and learn of me; for I am meek and lowly in heart: and ye shall find rest unto your souls. For my yoke is easy, and my burden is light." (Matthew 11:28-30).

Some people carry heavy loads that they believe God has laid on them. Others choose to carry their own loads. Although they are weary; they are convinced that no one can handle their responsibilities the way they can. They have great pride in their abilities and fail to recognize the capabilities of others.

There is also a lack of trust in God. We are not in the yoke alone; God is there too! He is willing and able to help us carry our burdens. God's yoke is easy and light! People suffer from physical and mental exhaustion. This is not God's will! God is displeased with us when we fail to enter into His rest. "Let us, therefore, be diligent to enter that rest..." (Hebrews 4:11).

THE GOOD WORD

By Evangelist Joyce Houseman

"Ruler Over Bondage"

Joseph was destined to be the most ill-fated of all the Old Testament characters. He was greatly loved by his father, who displayed his love by sewing a coat of many colors for his son. His father's love brought jealousy and hatred from his brothers. So much so, they wanted to murder him. Their hatred climaxed when Joseph shared a dream. In the dream, his brothers and his parents were bowing down to him.

A day came when Joseph's brothers tore from him the symbol of his father's love... the beautiful coat of many colors. His older brother, Reuben tried to intervene for Joseph's life, but his efforts failed when Joseph was sold by his other brothers to a passing caravan. Joseph was eventually sold in Egypt. You might think this was the end of Joseph's life; it was actually the beginning!

Joseph became an overseer of the house of the captain of the guards. Even though he was in bondage, his leadership qualities, and his godly character could not be diminished. The captain's wife, unfortunately, lusted after Joseph and became angry when he rejected her. Her anger led to lies, and as a result Joseph was thrown into prison. He remained there for several years, but even there, he was given a place of authority. Joseph had a gift of interpreting dreams; it was the interpretation of the King's dream that brought him from prison to the palace. He was made ruler in Egypt, second only to Pharaoh. A famine eventually brought him face to face with his brothers. He could have reacted to them with anger, but anger was not in his heart. He said, "You meant this for evil, but God meant it for good."

God used Joseph and his gift of interpreting dreams to understand, and save Egypt and Israel during a time of great famine. He had been in great bondage, but he became a ruler over it! You might be in a hard place too, but if you are faithful to God, He will be faithful to you. What Satan meant for your evil; God can turn for your good!

THE GOOD WORD

By Evangelist Joyce Houseman

"Starved to Death"

A man had been lost in the wilds for days without food. He had crawled within a short distance of help; however, he was not aware that help was nearby when he gave up and died. A news report said that two elderly people had starved to death in their home. Help was there, but they did not use it. Investigators found a fortune of money stuffed in drawers, clothing and other areas of their house.

There is an abundance of both natural and spiritual food in our country. A person starving to death because of natural hunger is rare; however, spiritual lack of nourishment is not rare. People fail to avail themselves of the riches at God's table. Bibles are plentiful, yet they sit on shelves, collecting dust. Some nibble at God's Word, but few devour and digest it. How can people expect to sustain their spiritual growth?

Shepherds of churches feed their flocks, yet only a small percentage attend. Churches are for more than marrying, burying, and holiday visits. God has provided us with a well-balanced meal; the milk, bread, fruit and meat of His Word, yet many do not know it is there. Some know, and will not partake... Very sad!

THE GOOD WORD

By Evangelist Joyce Houseman

"Strength is Made Perfect in Weakness"

A chain is only as strong as its weakest link. Paul had a weakness and prayed to be delivered from 'the thorn in his flesh' three times. Christ answered him saying, "My grace is sufficient for you; for my strength is made perfect in weakness." (2 Corinthians 12:19). Paul said the 'thorn in his flesh' had been given to keep him humble.

Paul was greatly used by God; yet, He recognized his weakness. He knew that with the strength of Christ, he could say, "When I am weak; then am I strong." (2 Corinthians 12:10). God can give power to people with weaknesses when they turn their lives over to Him. God can take our greatest weakness and make it the greatest point of His strength.

It is not our strength, abilities, or personality that make the difference. It is "Christ in you, the Hope of Glory" that makes 'ALL' the difference! If you are outside of Christ, your weakness can destroy you! Many of us do not have the ability to free ourselves from the weakness in our lives. Only Christ can do that. God can make something wonderful out of our lives when we turn our weaknesses and lives over to Him!

THE GOOD WORD

By Evangelist Joyce Houseman

"Study the Word"

A university student and I were talking about the Bible when he said, "I do not believe the Bible; it is filled with contradictions." After asking him what the contradictions were; he admitted that he had never read the Bible. It is amazing to me, that people who would never dream of rejecting other teachings; or who claim to be experts on subjects without extensive study, disregard the Word of God so easily!

Rejecting the Word of God is tragic. Rejecting it with an attitude of totality is a double tragedy. Another tragedy is claiming to believe the Word of God, yet never taking the time to study it. Many believers are in the same condition the Jews were in when they rejected Christ. They were blinded by the traditions of the elders; they did not know the Work of God!

It is not enough to know your church doctrine or to sit under Bible teachers. You must search the Word of God for yourself. "Study to show yourself approved unto God, a workman that needs not to be ashamed, rightly dividing the Word of truth." (2 Timothy 2:15). "Search the scriptures." (John 5:39). This means more than an occasional reading of a verse or a chapter. Some people claim they cannot understand the Word of God. The Bible says, "If our Gospel is hidden, it is hidden to them that are lost." (2 Corinthians 4:3). The Bible also says,"There is nothing hidden that will not be revealed." (Luke 8:17). When describing the things coming upon the earth in the last days, (Matthew 24). Christ said, "Be not deceived!"

If you have not been searching the Word of God, you will be deceived. When He, the Spirit of truth is come, He will guide you into all truth..." (John 16:13). The Holy Spirit makes alive the Word of God! Deception will not be able to stand against the Word of God.

THE GOOD WORD

By Evangelist Joyce Houseman

"The Crutch"

A church service was in progress in a small town when a drunk, smitten by his conscience, staggered up the steps. Not wishing to reveal his condition, he leaned against a door to steady himself. To his embarrassment, the door was a swinging door. It flung open, sending him backward down steps. Enemies of Christianity refer to Christianity as a crutch for the weak. Paul experienced the truth that 'The Spirit' of man is willing, but 'The flesh' of man is weak!

Christians are not ashamed to lean on Christ. We call it "Leaning on the everlasting arms." "The fool has said in his heart there is no God." (Psalm 14:1). "I am strong; I need nothing and no one." He leans too; however, the crutch he leans on leads to ruin; alcohol, drugs, the wrong crowd... These things offer no more holding power than the swinging door offered the drunk.

"God has chosen the foolish things of the world to confound the wise, and God has chosen the weak things of the world to confound the things which are mighty." "That no flesh should glory in His presence." (1 Corinthians 1:27, 29). Through Christ, it can be said, "Let the weak say I am strong." (Joel 3:10).

THE GOOD WORD

By Evangelist Joyce Houseman

"The Curse"

A great curse swept across our land. The devastation of it has been greater than any war, any plague, any earthquake or any storm. The curse I am referring to is the "Drug cult." It has swept countless numbers of young people into its clutches. Drug pushers have no mercy, no pity, and no conscience. They are consumed with sin and greed. Vast numbers of young people have overdosed, committed suicide and many have been murdered as a result of drugs.

Countless numbers of teens have been physically and mentally marred for life. Jails, prisons, psychiatric wards, and graves are filled because of the "Drug cult." One of my sons was in elementary school when a drug pusher offered him drugs on his school's playground. There are no age limits, and no neighborhoods that are off limit with this curse.

In one way or another, it has touched people of all ages, all backgrounds and all walks of life. Even innocent, unborn babies are affected by mothers who have taken drugs. Minds have been left damaged, depressed, and without drive or an ability to think clearly. Minds have become closed to reasonable thinking, thus leading to the power of satanic suggestion. It isn't God who tells a mom on drugs to place her baby in a microwave oven. It isn't God who tells a young person to jump off a balcony to their death because they can fly... Drugs have had a great impact on the rise in witchcraft, demon worship, and eastern religions.

"The coming of the *lawless one* is according to the working of Satan, with all power, signs, and lying wonders, and with all unrighteous deception among those who perish, because they did not receive the love of the truth, that they might be saved. And for this reason, God will send them strong delusion, that they should believe the lie, that they all may be condemned who did not believe the truth but had pleasure in unrighteousness." (2 Thessalonians 2:9-12).

No greater judgment could ever befall a nation than to lose an entire generation of youth to drugs. Police officers have called them "The lost generation!" If there was ever a time for America to cry out to God, it is now!

THE **GOOD WORD**

By Evangelist Joyce Houseman

"The Devil"

Some people ignore the existence of the devil. Others believe that ignoring him, will make him go away! The devil likes attention because he is very proud. His pride caused him to try to exalt himself above God. His pride led to his downfall, and to him becoming the devil. The devil is insensitive, so ignoring him, will not make him go away. "Woe to the inhabited of the earth and of the sea! For the devil is come down unto you, having great wrath, because he knows that he has but a short time." (Revelation 12:12).

"Be sober, be vigilant; because your adversary the devil, as a roaring lion, walks about, seeking whom he may devour." (1 Peter 5:8). If the devil can't get you with big problems, he will try to wear you out with numerous little things! "The little foxes corrupt the vine." (Solomon 2:15).

The devil is our enemy! He works through whoever will give him an open door. There are times when he will even work through fellow church-goers. Working through church-goers makes him harder to recognize, but he is behind every evil deed. It is difficult to recognize him when he appears as an angel of light.

Regardless of how he chooses to appear, "We wrestle not against flesh and blood, but against principalities, against powers, against the rulers of the darkness of this world, against spiritual wickedness in high places." (Ephesians 6:12). Within our own power, we are not a match for Satan! God knew this, so he gave us instructions in His Word: "... be strong in the Lord and in the power of his might. Put on the whole armor of God, that ye may be able to stand against the wiles of the devil." (Ephesians 6:10-11). Wear the whole armor of God, and Satan will NEVER be able to defeat you!

"The Armor of God"

By Carol Gebert

What is the whole armor of God? It is the spiritual armor that helps us stand strong against the enemy. **The belt of truth:** A belt holds everything together, so this is a very important part of your armor. Truth secures us. One of Satan's greatest offensive tactics are to deceive us; he is the father of lies. With the belt of truth, we can defend ourselves against his lies and deception. When we live a life of truth, honesty, and integrity, our belt of truth secures and keeps our spirituality intact. The truth is very freeing! The Bible says, "And you shall know the truth and the truth shall make you free." (John 8:32). God's Word is the truth!

Breastplate of Righteousness: The breastplate of righteousness covers our heart and other vital organs. The breastplate covers the most vulnerable areas of a warrior. "Watch over your heart with all diligence, for from it flow the springs of life." (Proverbs 4:23). The righteousness that guards a believer's heart is the righteousness of Christ. (2 Corinthians 5:21). Righteousness is living a moral and spiritual life that is pleasing to God.

Feet shod with the gospel of peace:
The peace that comes in knowing Christ makes our feet desirous to walk in whatever He has called us to. It helps us flee temptation. A scripture says, "How beautiful on the mountains are the feet of the one who brings news of peace, who announces good things, who announces salvation, who says to Zion, Your God reigns!" (Isaiah 52:7). My late husband's feet were truly shod with the gospel of peace. He took the gospel of Jesus Christ to places where many men would fear to go. Miles were walked weekly, as he handed out tracts and won souls to the Lord.

Shield of faith: The shield of faith is used to "extinguish all the flaming darts of the evil one" When Satan attacks us, our faith in Christ lessens the blow. We are able to withstand the attack because of our faith in God and His Word! My worst experience with flaming darts of the evil one was when I went through postpartum depression. If I had not known the Lord, I am sure I could have ended up in an institution.

Thank God for faith, and pray for those who have lost it. "Without faith, it is impossible to please God, for he that comes to God must believe that He is; and that He is a rewarder of them that diligently seek Him." (Hebrews 11:6). "Faith comes by hearing, and hearing by the Word of God!" (Romans 10:17). The more you read God's Word, the stronger your shield of faith will become. **Helmet of salvation:** The helmet protects our mind. "The mind of Christ is given to believers through the Spirit of God." Our mind is where battles take place. Many years ago, I read something that I never forgot. "We are not responsible for the thoughts the enter our mind; only the thoughts that we entertain." It is vitally important to immediately smite any thought that is contrary to God, and to His will for us. How can we smite it? With the Word of God! Even one or two scriptures can get the job done.

Years ago, fear gripped my mind! "God has not given me a spirit of fear, but of power and of love and of a sound mind." 2 Timothy 1:7 gave me the victory! "And be not conformed to this world: but be ye transformed by the renewing of your mind, that ye may prove what *is* that good, and acceptable, and perfect, will of God." Renew your mind in prayer and in God's Word. (Romans 12:2). Doing this will keep our helmet in place!

Sword of the Spirit: This is the Word of God! "For the Word of God *is* quick, and powerful, and sharper than any two-edged sword, piercing even to the dividing asunder of soul and spirit, and of the joints and marrow, and *is* a discerner of the thoughts and intents of the heart." (Hebrews 4:12). It must be read, studied, digested and spoken! I can tell you from personal experience that the Word of God is living, and powerful! You will win your battles against the enemy when you are armed with the Word of God! It is our ammunition! "For as the rain comes down, and the snow from heaven, and do not return there, but water the earth, and make it bring forth and bud, that it may give seed to the sower, and bread to the eater, so shall My word be that goes forth from My mouth; It shall not return to Me void, but it shall accomplish what I please, And it shall prosper *in the thing* for which I sent it." (Isaiah 55:10-11). This is a powerful portion of scripture. Knowing that we can speak the Word of God, and it will not return void... makes me want to shout it from the rooftops.

The "Sword of the Spirit" will also keep you from sin."Your Word have I hidden in my heart, that I might not sin against you." (Psalm 119:11) The Holy Spirit will bring God's Word to the forefront of your mind in times of temptation. The Holy Spirit will also bring you answers from the Word of God. Numerous times, I have been in situations where an answer was needed for myself or another person... and the answer instantaneously came into my mind. There is a scripture for absolutely every need, desire, and situation in life.

As you have read, every part of your armor is vital! Wear it, and you WILL have the victory in your war against the enemy of your soul!

THE **GOOD WORD**

By Evangelist Joyce Houseman

"The Greatest Price Ever Paid"

Everyone loves a bargain; however, we often get what we pay for. Bargains and sales will at times, consist of outdated, damaged or inferior merchandise. Christ desired to make the largest purchase ever made. The price was very high; no bargains, but it had to be paid. "We were not purchased with silver and gold, but with the precious blood of Jesus Christ. His blood and the torture that caused his blood to be shed, was the price that was paid for buying back humanity. We are "The purchased possession."

We had been sold into the hands of Satan in the garden thousands of years before this price was paid. Christ was the only one who could lay His life down to redeem us. He was without spot and wrinkle. He was without sin and guile. Only Christ, the only begotten son of God could be acceptable to God. He was the perfect sacrifice. Christ proved Himself on earth against every temptation known to man. He was the victor in a face to face confrontation with the devil. Even when it was hard, he endured the cross and despised the shame. He saw the joy that was set before Him in the redemption of all mankind.

"Do you not know that your body is the temple of the Holy Spirit *who is* in you, whom you have from God, and you are not your own? For you were bought with a price; therefore glorify God in your body and in your spirit, which are God's." (1 Corinthians 6:19-20). Greater love has no man than this. One day, Christ is coming to claim His purchase! "I will send my messenger, who will prepare the way before me. Then suddenly the Lord you are seeking will come to his temple; the messenger of the covenant, whom you desire, will come," says the LORD Almighty." (Malachi 3:1).

THE **GOOD WORD**

By Evangelist Joyce Houseman

"The Kingdom of Heaven"

"Repent Ye, for the Kingdom of Heaven, is at hand." This was the message of John the Baptist. Jesus came preaching the same message. Jesus instructed his disciples to preach the Kingdom message. Most of Jesus' teachings were concerning the Kingdom of Heaven. "Repent Ye, for the Kingdom of Heaven, is at hand!"

Scripture clearly tells us where the Kingdom of heaven is. "And when He was demanded of the Pharisees when the Kingdom of God should come, he answered them saying: "The Kingdom of God comes not with observation; neither shall they say, Lo here! Or Lo there! For behold the Kingdom of God is within you." (Matthew 17:20-21).

When Jesus was on earth, the people wanted to set Him up as a King, and would have done so by force, but Jesus was not interested in a natural throne. His desire was not to reign over men from without; His desire was to reign within the hearts of humankind. "As overcomers, we will sit on the throne with him; ruling over our own lives, instead of being ruled by our senses and desires.

This message is so important, Jesus taught His disciples more about it after he had risen from the dead; and before he ascended into heaven. The time was not yet for the fullness of the Kingdom to be set up, so He told them that the Holy Spirit would come to them. The Holy Spirit gave them power and truth to lead and guide them until His Kingdom was complete.

Jesus Christ had a purpose in teaching the Lord's Prayer. I believe it is one of the most powerful prayers we can pray. "Thy Kingdom come; Thy will be done in earth as it is in Heaven. For thine is the Kingdom and the power and the glory forever." The Gospel of the Kingdom shall be preached in all the world, and then, the end shall come.

THE GOOD WORD

By Evangelist Joyce Houseman

"The Prisoner"

The jailer put two men into the inner dungeon, and as a precautionary measure clamped their feet in the stocks. He made sure the prisoners would not escape. The heavy prison door slammed shut! Such actions would suggest the prisoners were criminals. No, they were not criminals at all! They were ministers of the Gospel of Jesus Christ. What a position for two men of God to find themselves in, yet, they were not discouraged. They were heard singing and praising God, all over the prison.

Prison was not a new experience for Paul. He had been imprisoned many times for preaching the Gospel message. He had also been beaten, stoned, shipwrecked, in danger, left for dead, hungry, cold, and naked. Paul was physically bound but spiritually free! Paul used his time in prison to write letters of encouragement and instruction to churches. His letters comprised many books of the Bible.

Churches in Paul's time and churches today, benefit greatly from Paul's prison time writings! Paul stated in the book of Ephesians that he was a prisoner of Jesus Christ. "To be a prisoner of Jesus Christ is to be free!" In (Galatians 5:1)

Paul wrote, "Stand fast in the liberty wherewith Christ hath made us free." Christ saw the bondage in the hearts and minds of all humanity. Christ came to set at liberty those who are bound. John 8:36 says, "If the son, therefore, shall make you free; you shall be free indeed." Paul, believed and accepted this wonderful truth; do you?

THE **GOOD WORD**

By Evangelist Joyce Houseman

"The Snake"

"At the last it bites like a serpent and stings like a viper." (Proverbs 23:32). Not long ago, I was in an emergency room at a large hospital. It was a hectic place to be, as a constant stream of people arrived for help. It was not easy to look upon the suffering of others. An unexpected commotion filled the emergency room when a one-legged, drunk man arrived. He was in need of treatment for a substantial number of self-inflicted knife wounds.

His crutches were taken, and he was placed on a gurney. Within minutes, a loud crashing sound was heard. The man had rolled off and was lying face down on the floor. He started sobbing and beating the floor with his fists. I was aware that he was not crying from his physical pain; he was crying from the painful suffering that he felt within.

He was carefully lifted off the floor. With a need to prevent another fall, the man was restrained and pushed to the side of the room. I watched as he pulled on his restraints. I walked over to him and said, "Do you know that Jesus loves you?" He became perfectly still and stared at me. I told him about the love of God, and how nothing can separate us from God's love. As I talked to him, I realized he was much younger that I had assumed. Sin had taken its toll! He seemed to sober up, as he hung his head in shame. I learned that he had studied to be a minister at one of our nation's finest Bible Colleges. He had fallen away from his calling when he decided to experiment with the so-called pleasures of sin.

Alcohol was not the pleasure that he had expected. It had placed a horrible grip on his life. Rather than becoming a minister; he became a resident of skid row. His situation had become so depressing, he wanted to end his life. He was willing to pray. We prayed together, and he recommitted his life to Christ. His spiritual wounds were healed that night. His physical wounds were treated, and he was transferred to a detox center.

There are over six million alcoholics in the United States. "Wine is a mocker, strong drink is raging whoever is deceived by it is not wise." (Proverbs 20:1). Alcohol has left his terrible mark on many lives. Hearts and bodies have been broken by its devastating grip. Alcoholism always starts with that first drink. If you do not take that first drink; you will not have to worry about the last drink.

THE GOOD WORD

By Evangelist Joyce Houseman

"The Will of God"

God's desire is to have His will in our lives. A wise person knows that God's will is best, even more so than our own will. God knows our future; He knows the outcome of all things! God worked great miracles for the children of Israel, yet, they frequently wanted their own way! "They soon forgot His works; They did not wait for counsel, but lusted exceedingly in the wilderness, and tested God in the desert. And He gave them their request but sent leanness into their soul." (Psalms 106:13-15)

They eventually wanted a King! A King was not God's will for them, but they insisted, so God let them have their way. The end result? They lost out! When we choose our will and way, over God's will and way, we will lose out! Jesus said, "My meat is to do the will of Him, that sent me." (John 4:34). Jesus Christ often said that He came not to do His will, but the will of His father who sent Him. Jesus obeyed God's will all the way to the cross. He prayed, "Father, if thou be willing, remove this cup from me, nevertheless, not my will, but thine be done."

Jesus said, "Whosoever shall do the will of my father, the same is my brother, my sister, and mother. In the Lord's prayer, He taught us to pray, "Thy Kingdom come, Thy will be done in earth as it is in Heaven." We please God when we set aside our will and desires for His will! Choosing God's will brings the blessings of God upon us! "In every thing give thanks: for this is the will of God in Christ Jesus concerning you." (1Thessalonians 5:18).

"I delight to do thy will, O my God: yea, thy law is within my heart." (Psalm 40:8).

THE **GOOD WORD**

By Evangelist Joyce Houseman

"The Work of Creation"

A man had a beautiful flower garden. Many hours were spent in producing lovely results. A passerby stopped to admire his garden. She said, "Isn't it wonderful... the flowers that God grows?" The man responded! "Yes, it is, but you should have seen this spot of land when God had it by Himself!" it was once stated: "God created the heaven and the earth, but He left the finishing touches to mankind."

When God created man, He placed within him the ability to create, and to carry on with the work of creation. God created all the resources known and unknown to mankind. He filled the earth, water, and air, with endless amounts of minerals and sources of energy. He gave man dominion over it all! He even let Adam name all of the animals. Adam certainly was creative when he came up with all of the names.

God made man to be a steward over everything on earth. He gave mankind resources and the ability to utilize them; however, in working these things, it takes the power of God and man working together. John's Gospel says, "Without Me, you can do nothing!" The work of creation continues... Great medical advances; scientific discoveries, artistic creations, a book, a song... Creativity is endless! Although they may not believe it, even the agnostics ability to invent, create and discover is done so by the power of God. These blessings are given to all, just as the rain and the sunshine are given to all.

God hid gold, silver, coal and oil in the earth. He also hid talents within each one of us. Mankind's talents, which come in vast varieties assist with the furtherance of creation. If we are wise, we will acknowledge God in all things, and thank Him for allowing us to have a part in it all!

'What is man that you are mindful of him?" (Psalm 8:4).

THE **GOOD WORD**

By Evangelist Joyce Houseman

"The Would Be Followers Of Christ"

Jesus remained in near obscurity for the first thirty years of His life. After years of preparation were completed; God placed His approval on His son! God's voice spoke from Heaven after Jesus was was water baptized. "Thou art my beloved son in whom I am well pleased." Soon after, Jesus chose his disciples, and His ministry was thrust into full force. His fame went into every area of His country. Miracles were performed by Jesus everywhere! The people had never seen anything like it.

The miracles and His fame caused many people to want to follow Him. One man said, "Lord, I will follow you wherever you go." Jesus answered him; "Foxes have holes and birds of the air have nests, but the son of man has nowhere to lay his head." A would-be-follower who was impressed by Jesus' fame, but opposed to the sacrifice and discomfort required in following Jesus, begged off when he said, "Let me first go and bury my father." A third person said, "Let me first go and bid them farewell, which are at home at my house."

A rich, young ruler came seeking after Jesus, and left in sorrow when Jesus told him to give all that he had to the poor. Jesus Christ was not insensitive to the feelings and needs of others; however, He knew the hearts of men better than they knew themselves. Followers dropped off and left Jesus, as His sayings became harder. The Bible says, "They walked no more with Him."

There are many would-be-followers of Jesus Christ today. Many seem to make a good start but turn back when the way starts getting a little hard. And Jesus said unto him, "No man having put his hand to the plow and looking back, is fit for the Kingdom of God."

THE **GOOD WORD**

By Evangelist Joyce Houseman

"The Wrong Road"

Travelers will at times, find themselves on wrong roads, going in wrong directions. This can easily happen when people do not read maps or road signs. At first, trips are taken with confidence and with complete assurance that everything is going to be just fine! Sometimes, miles have been driven before a person realizes that a mistake in direction has been made. Some routes are easy to recover. Some take miles and miles to correct.

Spiritually speaking, people lose their direction when they do not follow God's road map. I am referring to the Bible; the Holy Word of God! We might think we are doing just fine, but the Bible says, "There is a way that seems right to man, but the end are the ways of death." (Proverbs 14:12).

I know it is inconvenient and frustrating when a traveler has to backtrack after going in a wrong direction; however if they don't, they will get further and further away from their original, planned destination. Abraham was headed for a city whose builder and maker was God. He took a wrong direction and ended up in the bondage of Egypt. He corrected his path, and set his face like a flint towards that heavenly city. Sometimes, we have to humble ourselves and admit that we've taken the wrong road. Perhaps this has happened to you? Do not delay! Turn around; correct your path, and head in the right direction again! God is willing to help you. Just ask Him!

"Show me your ways, O Lord; Teach me your paths." (Psalm 25:4).

"trust in the Lord with all your heart, and lean not on your own understanding; in all your ways acknowledge Him, and He shall direct your paths." (Proverbs 3:5-6).

THE GOOD WORD

By Evangelist Joyce Houseman

"There is Hope"

Inflation; polluted and depleted energies, an increase in crime, unemployment, and lack of peace in the world, have caused people to lose hope. When we lack in understanding of God's Word, it is easy to develop a fatalistic attitude or, an attitude that says, 'what is the use?'

Scripture in the book of Jeremiah states that God is the hope of Israel and that God was Jeremiah's own personal hope in the time of evil. Our hope begins to fail when we fail to realize that God is God! And that he is in control of everything! The Bible tells us that God's throne is in the heavens, and His footstool is the earth. He sits in a place of complete authority over everything! Everything under His feet is under His control. Even Satan can only go as far as God allows.

"Have you not known? Have you not heard? The everlasting God, the LORD, the Creator of the ends of the earth, neither faints nor is weary? Isaiah 40:28

If you are losing your hope; perhaps it is because you are placing your hope on the wrong things. There is a song that says, "My hope is built on nothing less than Jesus' blood and righteousness. I dare not trust the sweetest frame but wholly lean on Jesus' name. On Christ the solid rock I stand, all other ground is sinking sand."

"The Lord is my rock and my fortress and my deliverer; My God, my strength, in whom I will trust; My shield and the horn of my salvation, my stronghold." (Psalm 18:2).

THE GOOD WORD

By Evangelist Joyce Houseman

"Treasurers"

"We brought nothing into this world and it is certain we can carry nothing out." (1 Timothy 6:7). After hearing about the death of a well-to-do man, a neighbor asked, 'What did he leave?" The answer was, "He left everything!" Another neighbor spoke up. "The way he pursued wealth; I thought hc might havc found a way to take it with him." A humorous conversation perhaps, yet, scriptures concerning wealth are not humorous.

The Bible tells us in (Luke 8:14) "Now the ones that fell among thorns are those who, when they have heard, go out and are choked with cares, riches, and pleasures of life, and bring no fruit to maturity." The Word of God is choked out of the hearts of people who are in this condition.

"Lay not up for yourselves treasures upon earth where moth and rust do corrupt, and where thieves break through and steal: But lay up for yourselves treasures in heaven, where neither moth nor rust doth corrupt, and where thieves do not break in and steal: For where your treasure is, there will your heart be also." (Matthew 6:19).

God knows that we need to provide for ourselves and our families. (Timothy 5:8) says, "But if any provide not for his own, and especially for those of his own house, he has denied the faith and is worse than an infidel." Provide and set some aside for your future, but do not forget to invest in the reserve bank of heaven. It is the safest place, and it pays the best interest!

THE GOOD WORD

By Evangelist Joyce Houseman

"Victory Over Temptation"

"No temptation has overtaken you except such as is common to man; but God *is* faithful, who will not allow you to be tempted beyond what you are able, but with the temptation will also make the way of escape, that you may be able to bear *it.*" (1 Corinthians 10:13). Temptation has been here since the beginning of time. It was Eve's inability to overcome temptation that caused humanity's fall in the garden. Satan uses the weapon of temptation to war against the mind and body.

Regardless of how strong a person seems to be; there isn't anyone who is free from temptation. Even Christ was in all points tempted as we are, yet, He was without sin. (Hebrews 4:15). Satan temps our flesh through our five senses. Those things that would satisfy the flesh without regards to the cost. The real culprit; however, is not temptation; it is lust! Temptation becomes powerful when lust is in a person's life. "But every man is tempted when he is drawn away of his own lust and enticed. Then when lust has conceived; it brings forth sin. When it is finished; it brings forth death." (James 1:14-15).

Sin is in the heart of man and only needs temptation to bring it forth. Jesus Christ was sinless, so temptation had no power over him. David prayed, "Create within me a clean heart and renew within me, a right spirit." If we will allow Christ to cleanse our heart, we will come to a place in Christ where it will become pointless for Satan to try to tempt us. There will not be anything left for him to work on. Through Jesus Christ, there is the victory over every temptation. He faced temptations of every kind and came out the victor! You can have an overcoming life of victory too!

"I can do all things through Christ who strengthens me." (Philippians 4:13).

THE GOOD WORD

By Evangelist Joyce Houseman

"Water"

In recent years we learned that water can no longer be taken for granted. Our supply became depleted through pollution and waste. This was a wake-up call that caused great concern. There are many people who take our religious freedom for granted too. The local church; Gospel Radio and TV programs, religious literature, will always be available, right?

"Behold the days come says the Lord God, that I will send a famine in the land; not a famine of bread, nor thirst for water, but of hearing the Words of the Lord. And they shall wander from sea to sea, and from the north even to the east, they shall run to and fro to seek the Word of the Lord, and shall not find it. In that day shall the fair virgins and young men faint for thirst." (Amos 8:11-13).

A person can live for a time without food, but only a very short time without water. A starving person can lose their hunger, but never their thirst. When on the cross, Jesus did not ask for food. He said, "I thirst." David described his desire for God when he said, "As the deer pants for streams of water, so my soul pants for You, my God." (Psalms 42:1).

I lived on a farm during my growing up years. I can remember using a hand pump to fill buckets of water. A deer can empty a bucket of water in a few seconds. It takes up to six buckets to satisfy their thirst. The Bible describes our spiritual desires as thirst.

Jesus said, "If any man thirst, let him come unto me, and drink. There is a pure river of life flowing to humankind. As you drink of this spiritual water; it will flow in and through you to others who are thirsty... It will bring them life as well. Avail yourself to the water of life, while there is still an opportunity to do so.

THE GOOD WORD

By Evangelist Joyce Houseman

"What is in a Name?"

According to the Word of God, a person's name is of great importance. In Bible days, a name was frequently given to fit the nature of a person. Abraham was originally called Abram. His wife Sarah was originally called Sarai. God changed their names after he changed their natures. God dealt with Jacob for years before changing his name to Israel to fit his new nature.

There was a stir when naming, John the Baptist. An Angel sad, "Thou shalt call his name John." People became disturbed because there weren't any family members named John. Elizabeth heeded the instruction of the Angel, and said, "His name is John." People turned to the father for an answer. He agreed by saying, "His name is John."

The name John represented what John would become; a great prophet, bringing the knowledge of salvation to the people, and bringing people out of darkness into the glorious light. He was also the forerunner of Jesus Christ. (Luke 2:21) tells us that Jesus was named before he was conceived in the womb. (Isaiah 9) says, "He is wonderful; a counselor, the mighty God, the everlasting Father, the Prince of Peace. There is authority in the name of Jesus, for "The government shall be upon His shoulders. And of His peace and government, there is no end." "The name of Jesus is above all other names." A time will come when "At the name of Jesus, every knee will bow and every tongue will confess that he is Lord."

What is in a name? At the name of Jesus, the devil trembles. When you approach the throne of God, and you mention the name of Jesus, the gates of heaven are opened to you! Jesus is King of Kings and Lord of Lords! There is no other name given under heaven whereby men can be saved.

THE **GOOD WORD**

By Evangelist Joyce Houseman

"When Saw We thee?"

And the King will answer and say to them, 'Assuredly, I say to you, inasmuch as you did it to one of the least of these My bretheran, you did it to Me.' (Matthew 25:40). The true mark of a Christian is found in how much they care for others. It is not enough to say, "I love God; I love humanity!" We show our love for God in the way we treat our fellow man. I am not just referring to people who treat us well, or family and church members. I am referring to people who are needy.

Jesus said, "for I was hungry, and you gave Me food; I was thirsty, and you gave Me drink; I was a stranger, and you took Me in; I was naked, and you clothed Me; I was sick, and you visited Me; I was in prison, and you came to Me." People who see to the needs of others, do not realize that their love, compassion and kindness is being done for Christ.

There is a sharp line drawn between people who Jesus called sheep and goats. People who respond to the needs of others are 'The sheep.' Jesus said, "They shall inherit the Kingdom prepared for them." Goats are people who pass by the needy unconcerned. They have an

59

attitude that says, 'I have enough problems of my own.' Neglect of the needy is serious. Jesus said, 'Goats will go into everlasting punishment.' The way we treat others is the same way we treat Christ.

People who help others, help themselves. Scripture says, "Give, and it will be given to you: good measure, pressed down, shaken together, and running over will be put into your bosom. For with the same measure that you use, it will be measured back to you." (Luke:38).

THE **GOOD WORD**

By Evangelist Joyce Houseman

"You Cannot Legislate Love"

People in positions of authority have worked at bringing people together in understanding and love. Their efforts have been commendable, but not very effective. Prejudice and hatred seem deeper than it has ever been. People cannot be forced together because that does not create an atmosphere of love.

The source of man's love does not come from without; it comes from within the heart of man. I am referring to the heart that Christ dwells within. Ephesians says, "That Christ may dwell in your heart by faith; then you are rooted and grounded in love."

Rejecting God, is also rejecting the love of Christ within. The Bibles says,"The heart is desperately wicked; it is more deceitful than anyone can imagine." The book of Exodus tells us that God gave people ten laws to live by. Mankind did not live up to His laws, so God sent His only son to the cross to die for mankind. When Jesus was nailed to the cross, he fulfilled every written ordinance; and the laws were nailed to the cross with Him.

After that, God's law was placed in the hearts of whoever accepted Christ. God's law is the law of Love! That is why Christ could say to us "Love one another as I have loved you; and love your neighbor as yourself." Lawmakers made laws that took prayer and Bible reading out of schools. Any nation that thinks they can bring a peaceful coexistence without God is mistaken. God is love, and love is God!

Joyce and members of the "Victory Band."

"Speak to one another with psalms, hymns and spiritual songs. Sing and make music in your heart to the Lord." (Ephesians 5:19).

25734952R00037

Made in the USA
San Bernardino, CA
10 November 2015